D0080960

secular and sacred

SECULAR AND

sacred

Photographs of Mexico

Van Deren Coke

Introduction by Tony Cohan

UNIVERSITY OF NEW MEXICO PRESS

Albuquerque

WITHDRAWN

BOWLING GREEN STATE
UNIVERSITY LIBRARIES

Acknowledgments

I want to thank Joan, my wife, for helping to select the pictures chosen for reproduction and for contributing valuable suggestions about the texts. I feel that Tony Cohan's introduction captures the spirit of my intentions and the human dimension that compelled me to make these pictures in the country both of us always find fascinating. It was Carmen Masip de Hawkins of San Miguel de Allende, Mexico, who started me thinking about making a book of my photographs of that country. For this I am grateful; she caused me to rethink how I could present these images to a larger number of people in both the United States and Mexico than would have been possible by exhibitions alone. I want to express my appreciation to Milenda Nan Ok Lee for her imaginative design for the book and to Dana Asbury for her continued interest and advice during all levels of conception and production of this publication.

This book has its origins in an exhibition of Van Deren Coke's photographs organized by the University of New Mexico Art Museum. After its presentation in Albuquerque August 4–September 29, 1991, "Streets of Mexico: Photographs by Van Deren Coke" traveled to the Harwood Foundation in Taos, the College of Santa Fe, and the Roswell Museum and Art Center. The assistance of the University Art Museum in bringing this book to fruition is gratefully acknowledged.

Library of Congress Cataloging-in-Publication Data

Coke, Van Deren, 1921–
    Secular and sacred : photographs of Mexico / Van Deren Coke : introduction by Tony Cohan.
— 1st ed.
        p.   cm.
    ISBN 0-8263-1379-5
    1. Photography, Artistic.   2. Mexico—Social life and customs—Pictorial works.   I. Title.
TR654.C5998   1992
779′.9972—dc20
92-15219
CIP

Copyright © 1992 by the University of New Mexico Press
All rights reserved.
First edition

Printed and bound in Japan

contents

To the people of Mexico

introduction

In July of 1923, having written repeatedly to Alfred Stieglitz of his despair and feeling of stasis in California, Edward Weston left for Mexico "to start life anew, why I hardly know. . . ." There he entered an inspired creative period among artist friends, his lover Tina Modotti, and a culture that fascinated him endlessly. Photographing friends, nature, the landscape, and folk objects, Weston probed beneath Mexico's dazzling visual surfaces to arrive at a deeper empathy with form and subject. He experimented for the first time with still life, especially Mexican folk toys, *juguetes*. His work achieved new clarity and power, and was instantly acclaimed in Mexico. But by the end of 1926, emotionally exhausted and financially desperate, Weston returned to California.

Twelve years later he was visited by a young aspiring Kentucky photographer, Van Deren Coke. Entranced by Weston's Mexico photos and his collection of folk art, Coke undertook his own extended stay in Mexico in 1948, commencing an artistic preoccupation that would never wane. Like Weston before him, Coke would find in the country to the south a bottomless source of inspiration.

Fittingly, in 1983 it would be Coke—then director of the department of photography at the San Francisco Museum of Modern Art—who would sponsor the first in-depth show of Weston's Mexico photographs. In his catalog introduction, Coke wrote how Weston "turned the seductive light of Mexico into an agency that separated and abstracted masses, just as had the ancient Indian sculptors and architects." Weston struggled, Coke wrote, to "make out of the raw reality a photograph that was not romantic or picturesque . . . there was always an emphasis on the structural aspects of nature . . . a blend of realism and abstraction." In Weston's photographs of folk toys, Coke wrote, we sense "the haunting history of each object."

Coke might well have been writing these words about his own Mexico work.

Mexican life does not appear to us as a temporal event walled off from death, nor as a succession of discrete moments, but rather as a continuum in which forces emerge from dark and return to it. This quality invariably fascinates but often confounds and finally defeats most American and European artists, eager to isolate elements of space and time, to snatch figure from ground, light from dark, life from death. Mexico will not yield its soul so easily to this artistic appropriation, and few Western artists in any medium have managed to avoid the pitfalls of either glib romanticism on the one hand, or arrogant colonial assumptions on the other.

This problem of "the exotic" presents special challenges for the photographer. Weston spoke of his "fight to avoid [Mexico's] natural picturesqueness." Van Deren Coke has met this issue head on, shaping an honest, integral body of work that neither condescends to its subject nor adulates it. In the midst of a vigorous career in the United States as photographer, curator, museum director, and educator, Coke has returned time and again to haunt the lake villages of Pátzcuaro, walk the cobbled lanes of San Miguel de Allende, and visit the mountain communities and churches around Oaxaca. In his explorations along Mexico City's thronged Calle Madero, at bullfights and fiestas, in rural markets and lanes, Coke has evolved a method that allows him to abstract and to decontextualize the seemingly familiar into something startling, illuminating. At the same time, in his refusal to manipulate the image, Coke has left inviolate the purity of his subject, its mystery and form. While honoring the locality of his subject, he reveals its universal and enduring nature.

Gradually, out of this Mexican landscape of staggering visual abundance, of intense light and shadow, Coke has forged a unique photographic language—familiar yet unexpected, mysterious yet decipherable, formal yet spontaneous. In the collection of photographs presented here, taken since 1978, he has engaged as well the complex issue of color, developing the signature Cibachrome—with its heightened blacks and sudden bursts of red—into a distinctive revelatory tool.

It has often been said that Mexico's blend of natural extravagance, pre-Colombian mysticism, and Spanish culture is intrinsically "surrealistic." Reason is confounded at every turn, the logical eye left begging by the sudden juxtapositions. "Unconscious" material erupts continually into daily life. Frida Kahlo, accompanying her husband Diego Rivera to prewar Paris, reportedly found Europe's brand of drawing-room Surrealism bland, timid, inferior to the spectacle of everyday Mexican life.

No wonder then that European Surrealists came to Mexico as to an artistic Lourdes. In 1938 the poet and painter André Breton, following the earlier visit of French visionary dramatist Antonin Artaud, arrived in Mexico City. Breton, leader and custodian of Surrealism, wrote effusively of his impressions.

I had never heard the unalterable chants of Zapotec musicians, my eyes were blind to the extreme nobility, the extreme vulnerability of the Indian people, immobile in the sunlight of the markets. I could not imagine that the world of fruit could include a marvel such as the *pitahaya,* the pulp of which is colored and curled like a rose petal; the *pitahaya* whose flesh tastes like a kiss saturated with love and desire. I had never held in my hand a lump of that red earth from which come the painted statuettes of Colima, part woman and part cicada. And finally, I had not been vouchsafed that apparition, Frida Kahlo de Rivera, who like the shaft of light shed by the *quetzal,* scatters opals on the stones she passes.

4

Breton arrived in Mexico the same year Van Deren Coke visited Edward Weston in California—a coincidence perhaps worth noting. In 1940, with the help of Mexican and European painters and writers, Breton organized the "International Surrealist Exhibition" at the Gallery of Mexican Art. Other European artists, writers, and intellectuals followed, finding in Mexico a safe haven from fascism and persecution. A loosely knit group of European and indigenous Surrealists evolved, including among others the painters Leonora Carrington, Remdios Varo, and Frida Kahlo, and the writer Octavio Paz. In fact the Surrealist spirit thrived in Mexico for several decades more, well after it had ebbed in the U.S. and Europe. Never far from the reality of Mexican life and art, Surrealism continues to assert itself even today in the work of such contemporary Mexican artists as Francisco Toledo and Pedro Friedeberg.

One cannot look long at Van Deren Coke's eerily expressive folk toys, mysterious slashes of arrested life, eye-stopping collisions of object and form, before the adjective *surreal* floats to mind. "I always court enigma," Coke has said in reference to his photographs, and indeed his work inclines toward the bizarre, the fantastic, the seemingly improbable—departing in this fundamental regard from Weston's more lyric, classical approach.

While Coke's technique and aesthetics are informed by the entire history of twentieth-century photography, these Mexico photographs stand as, among other things, a strong addition to the unique, brilliant Mexican

Surrealist tradition—though Coke's Surrealism bears a more North American stamp: less calculated, more direct. One could speculate that as a young man in Mexico Coke first experienced that deep eruption of the unconscious that enabled him to sunder the constraining bonds of small-town American practicality and logic, and essay a leap into the territory of art. Mexico has always held out to the "gringo" artist what the Mediterranean south offered the northern European: the rich nectar of inspiration, and release for the thirsting soul.

Most important, Coke has squarely engaged the Mexico photographer's (and Surrealism's) central paradox: It is not the apparent world, but the one lurking behind it, that counts—the face behind the mask, the world of the invisible.

In a remarkable essay, "Seeing and Using: Art and Craftsmanship," Octavio Paz has written admiringly of Mexican folk objects. "Their beauty," Paz says, "is inseparable from their function: they are handsome because they are useful. Handicrafts belong to a world existing before the separation of the useful and the beautiful. . . . Utensil, talisman, symbol: beauty was the aura surrounding the object, the consequence—nearly always involuntary—of the secret relation between its making and its meaning."

He goes on to speak of "a physical presence that enters us through our senses and in which the principle of usefulness is constantly violated in favor of tradition, imagination, and even sheer caprice. . . . It lives in complicity with our senses, and that is why it is so hard to get rid of it—it is like throwing a friend out of the house. . . .

"Craftsmanship," Paz concludes, "is a sort of fiesta of the object: it transforms a utensil into a sign of participation."

Coke, an avid and long-standing collector of Mexican folk toys, *juguetes,* has repeatedly turned his eye to these strange objects, and they are surely among his most arresting images. In some cases the folk objects are shot where they are found—in markets, at fiestas—while others are formally staged still lifes (*naturaleza muerta*). In both instances, they draw us into a provocative, unsettling domain.

Coke's *juguetes* exist in a curious nether realm, like old dolls, or the eerie, Gothic art of Poe or German fairy tales. Cheerful and grim at the same time, like a Day of the Dead festival in any Mexican town, they quiver between life and death, waking and dream, suspended in the vibratory grid of the photograph. Imbued with a heightened drama and sense of occasion, they seem to suggest something just beyond our conscious comprehension—sinister perhaps, or just playful. The photographs lavish appreciation and wonder upon these objects, invoking traces of their origins and their strange histories, and often illuminating or suggesting their makers' editorial commentaries on life, death, politics, and society.

Coke has pointed out that "the biggest problem with photography is that you can gulp it down without digesting it." The jaded eye, glutted with images, has to be lured into engagement. As a strategem, shooting the *juguete* slows the eye down, drawing the viewer into a not-easily-digestible set of enigmas—artistic, social, even religious. Redolent of time and mystery and unseen origins, these photographs force the eye to linger, the senses to savor, the mind to drift into other possibilities. In this way Coke tricks the intractable limits of the photo, its quick decay toward superficiality, defeating the hasty glance by mesmerizing us.

Coke himself has written of the folk objects: "Whether hand-shaped or molded, these modern pieces reflect a love of nature, a sense of humor, and a marvelous understanding of how to articulate a surface to make it visually exciting. Contemporary Mexican folk ceramics . . . give us the feeling that we are close to the people who made and decorated these candelabra, pots, human and animal forms, and toys. . . . In their presence we are inspired to think differently about the commonplace as well as the fantastic."

Faces and masks. Cheerful grinning *calaveras* (skeletons). A festive Day of the Dead altar. A blind man with a blue cup. A statue of a Virgin with an eroding skull. "The connections between the images occur," Coke writes, "when they are seen not as individual vignettes, but as frames from a film fused into a metaphor."

From the profound blacks of these prints emerge fleeting, exact visions of light and life—almost as if a match had been briefly stuck on a moonless night to reveal an unsuspected region, fecund and teeming, directly in one's path. Coke's photographs, drawn out of a rich vein of continuous life, do not rescue their images from time but rather point back to the elemental and highly charged landscape from which they arise. In the act of mirroring a world they become a part of that world. Van Deren Coke has arrived at a deep, expressive metaphor of Mexican mystery.

Tony Cohan
San Miguel de Allende, Mexico

plates

Shirt Mannequin, Mexico City, 1983.

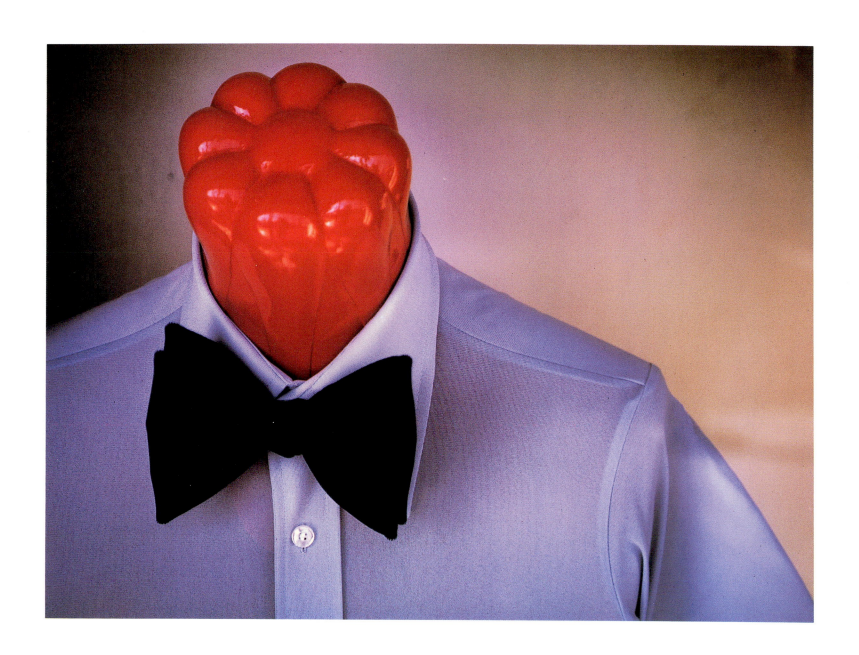

Store Window, Mexico City, 1987.

Head of a Ceramic Fiesta Figure, Ocatlán, Oaxaca, 1990.

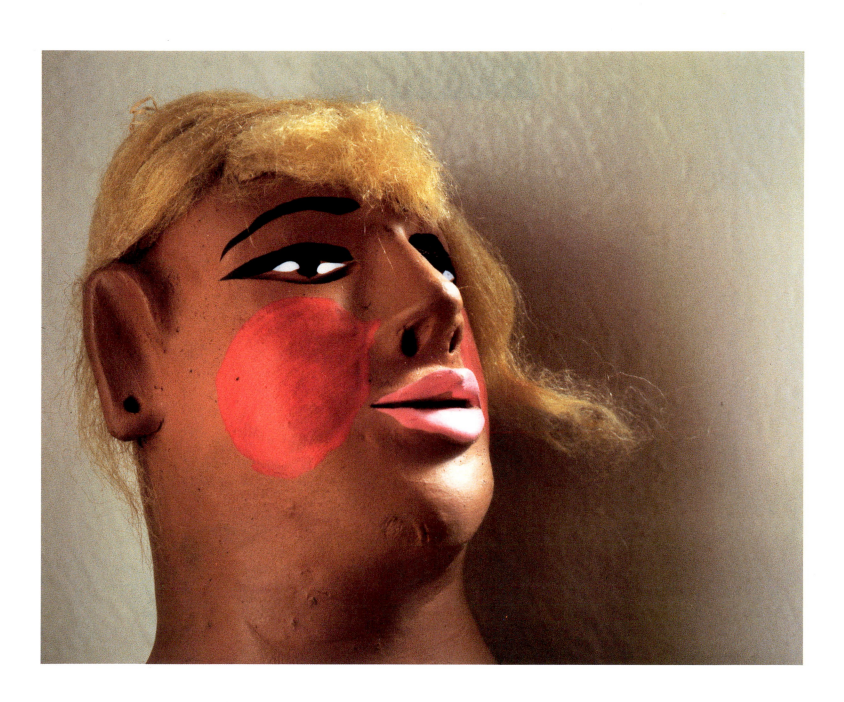

Ceramic Pieces, Santa Cruz de las Huertas, 1985.

Wooden Horse Used as a Prop by a Street Photographer, Guadalajara, 1991.

Papier-mâché Dolls and Masks, San Miguel de Allende, 1990.

Disassembled Puppet, Mexico City, 1988.

Broken Ceramic Pieces, Acatlán, Puebla, 1990.

Bicycle Seat, Tlaxcala, 1990.

Chairs on the Sidewalk, Quiroga, 1988.

Birds for Sale, Pátzcuaro Market, Pátzcuaro, 1992.

Carousel Horses, Yuriria, Mexico, 1992.

A Car in a Traveling Carousel, Cholula, 1987.

Papier-mâché Hobby Horse's Head, Celaya, 1980.

Car Mirrors for Sale at a Gas Station near Matamoros, Puebla, 1990.

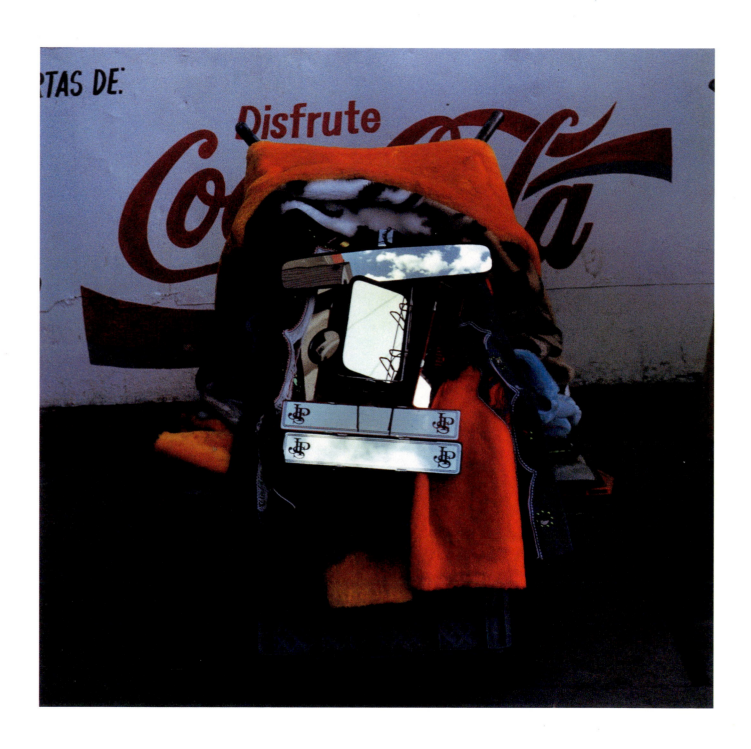

Boy Carrying Water on Construction Job, San Miguel de Allende, 1990.

Students After School, San Miguel de Allende, 1985.

Young Girl Bringing Home Firewood, San Miguel de Allende, 1985.

Boy Resting at Construction Job, San Miguel de Allende, 1991.

Students, San Miguel de Allende, 1988.

Young Girl Selling Tomatoes, San Miguel de Allende, 1982.

The way in which the young vendor is piling up her tomatoes goes back to pre-Hispanic times. We can see this practice illustrated in the early codices. When I first went to Mexico in 1948, one would never see a young girl with her lips thickly covered with lipstick. This is one of many changes taking place under the influence of mass merchandising, access to more periodicals, and exposure to television.

Man Buying Tomatoes, Pátzcuaro, 1988.

Young Girl Selling Tomatoes and Chilis, San Miguel de Allende, 1988.

Tomato Seller, Pátzcuaro, 1982.

Ceramic Pulque Jug and Its Shadow, Barrio de la Luz, Puebla, 1984.

Pulque has long been a popular inexpensive alcoholic drink in Mexico. It is a strong drink derived from fermented juice of the *maguey* plant, and if consumed in excess may cause ordinary objects to appear both very large and menacing.

A Memorial Bronze Head, Mexico City, 1984.

Small Ceramic Wall Planter in the Form of a Man's Head, Tzintzuntzán, 1981.

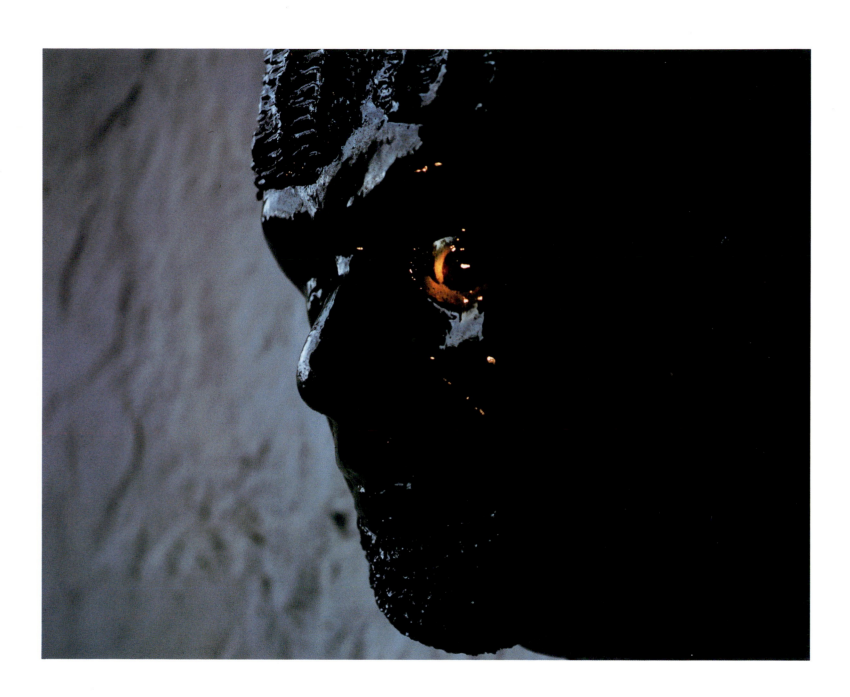

Fruits for Sale, San Miguel de Allende, 1988.

Artists with Their Work, Flea Market, Mexico City, 1989.

Mexico City Flea Market, 1984.

Old Family Portraits and a Tea Cup, Flea Market, Mexico City, 1978.

Blind Man with Blue Cup, San Miguel de Allende, 1985.

Each day this blind man sits outside of the post office in San Miguel de Allende, cup in hand, hoping to hear the clink of change left over from the purchase of stamps. The void of black gives this image an edge of menace, but my main intention was to convey in this emotionally charged subject a feeling that we are all in one way or another blind, without minimizing or romanticizing the effects of blindness.

Woman with a Cane Waiting to Cross the Street, San Miguel de Allende, 1988.

An Elderly Man and Woman Shopping in a Street Market,
San Miguel de Allende, 1990.

Street Musicians Begging, Mexico City, 1980.

Libertad Market, Guadalajara, 1991.

"Wellcome," Nogales, 1979.

Food Vendor, San Miguel de Allende, 1989.

Woman Wearing a Red Rebozo, San Miguel de Allende, 1980.

Waiting to Cross Canal Street, San Miguel de Allende, 1991.

Waiting for a Bus, San Miguel de Allende, 1989.

Two Men Repairing a Wall, San Miguel de Allende, 1987.

A Welding Shop Beside a Shop That Sells Handmade Cooking
Vessels, near Tlaxcala, 1990.

A Man Who Transports Food in Boxes Balanced on His
Head, San Miguel de Allende, 1980.

A Crippled Man Who Has Had a Lot to Drink, Resting, near Moralia, 1990.

A Beggar with Her Child Under Her Reboza, Guadalajara, 1990.

Lunch, Xochimilco, 1989.

Vendors sell hot corn on the cob all over Mexico. The red covering is a mixture of salt and red chile to add an agreeably sharp quality to the cooked corn.

Female Mule Driver, San Miguel de Allende, 1982.

Election Year, San Miguel de Allende, 1990.

Man with Goat, Erongaricuaro, Michoacán, 1979.

This photograph represents one of the rare instances when I wanted to make a political statement. The Mexican is pulling a goat behind him. The goat stands in my mind for Mexico, which is reluctantly moving toward a multiparty system of elections. The wall behind this drama is covered with political slogans and party logos. The PRI, which has controlled the election process since the early 1930s, is today giving way to candidates from the PAN party, a conservative, Catholic Church coalition. In a few cases in the last year or so, this party has won municipal elections and made a strong showing at the level of states' governors. One can also see the hammer and sickle logo of Mexico's small Communist party.

Bullfight, Mexico City, 1986.

Gored Bullfighter, Mexico City, 1986.

I took this photograph at a *novilladas* (apprentice bullfight). The bullfighters that afternoon included a young woman who was gored and had to be carried from the ring and a flashy but unwise matador who allowed the bull to take his cape away. Bullfighting at an amateur level illustrates how dangerous this activity is, a fact largely overlooked when the top matadors take to the ring.

Clean-up Men at a Bull Ring, Mexico City, 1986.

Dentist Office, Mexico City, 1982.

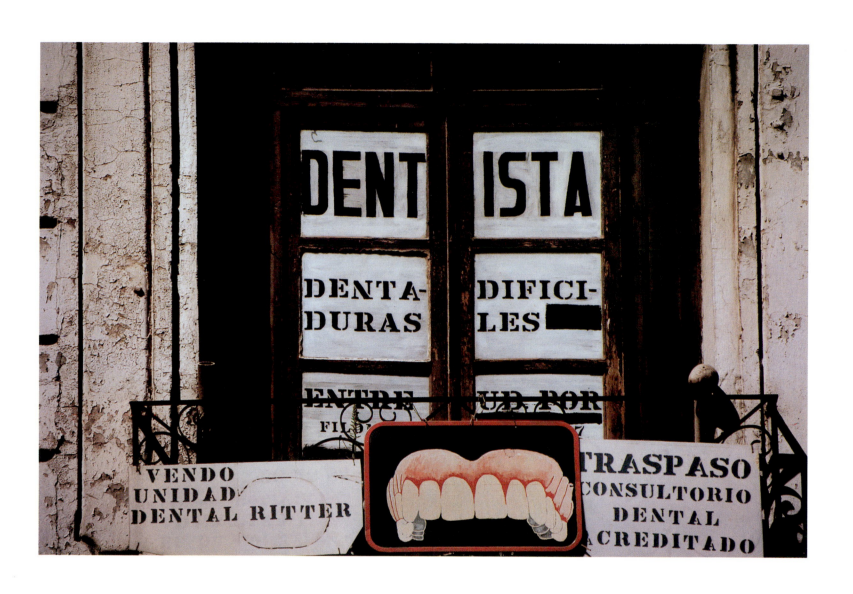

Hand Prints, San Miguel de Allende, 1985.

Barber Shop, Oaxaca, 1982.

Decoration on Plywood Fence Around Land Cleared After Earthquake-Damaged
Building Was Torn Down, Mexico City, 1992.

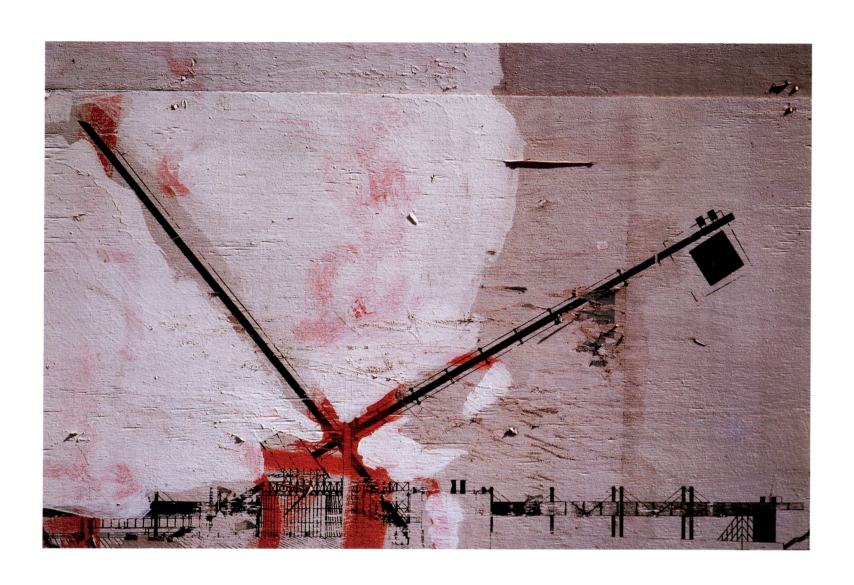

Cross Painted on a Column, San Miguel de Allende, 1985.

Nativity in Painted Tin, San Miguel de Allende, 1992.

Figures of the Virgin and St. Joseph Stored in an Adobe Barn, Solidad, 1989.

Women Straining Clay to be Shaped into Kiln-fired Vessels, Tecomatepec, 1990.

Christmas Decorations, Mexico City, 1988.

The Virgin Mary with a Shadow Across Her Chin Becoming a Bearded
Jesus Christ, Mexico City, 1980.

Detail of a Life-size Figure of Christ at the Post, Taxco, 1982.

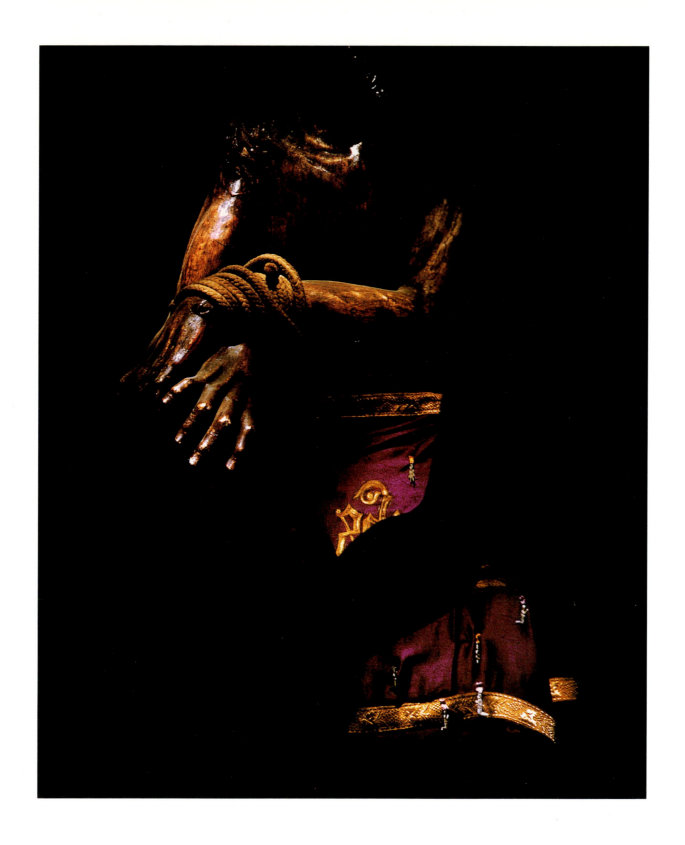

Figure of Christ for Sale, Mexico City, 1990.

Corpus Christi Parader Pushing a Paleta Cart, San Miguel de Allende, 1990.

The traditional procession held in San Miguel de Allende during the celebration of Corpus Christi (*Jueves de Corpus*) is an opportunity for dressing up in all kinds of costumes. Musical groups riding and performing on flatbed trucks are joined by individuals masked and costumed in fantastic parade garb. Each participant pays a fee to the consortium of churches that organizes the parade which winds through many of the spectator-crowded streets in the center of the city.

Corpus Christi Parader with Toy Horn, San Miguel de Allende, 1990.

Corpus Christi Parader, San Miguel de Allende, 1990.

January Fiesta Marchers, 1992.

Each January the people living in the villages on or near the ranches located in the countryside around San Miguel de Allende come to this their nearest city to celebrate their devotion to the Virgin of Guadalupe. They parade through the streets in all kinds of costumes led by the spirited sounds of brasses and drums. Members of the group, dressed as their Indian ancestors did in earlier times, perform dances that have their origins in the pre-Hispanic period.

Miniature Papier-mâché Death Mask on a Day of the Dead Ceramic
Candle Holder, Mexico City, 1978.

Day of the Dead Papier-mâché Fireworks Figures, San Miguel de Allende, 1992.

A Wooden Death Mask, Pátzcuaro, 1988.

Entrance to a Master Ceramic Worker's Studio, Metepec, 1984.

Funeral Procession, Pozos, 1982.

Marigolds for Day of the Dead Altar, November 1,
San Miguel de Allende, 1985.

This elderly man is probably a widower, for it is usually the women who buy bunches of marigolds, whose petals are used to decorate the altars set up in homes to commemorate the Day of the Dead in Mexico.

afterword

My first extended stay in Mexico took place in 1948. I had some feeling for the country, for my mother and father had made three trips to Mexico in the early 1930s and had brought back rugs, light fixtures, and ceramic pieces for our home in Lexington, Kentucky. At about the time of their trips south of the border I first met Edward Weston in Carmel, California, in the summer of 1938. He generously spent hours showing this then teenager a broad selection of his prints. I was especially impressed by those done in Mexico. As a consequence, he introduced me to his collection of Mexican folk art objects, many of which had been subjects for pictures made when he lived in Mexico in the mid 1920s. Both his pictures and the humble artifacts fascinated me then and continue to do so today.

Weston resisted photographing the exotic aspects of the country such as the flowers, fog in the mountains, and the charming Indian children. The moody feeling of incipient violence was also missing. What he did pin down were the ever-changing patterns of light and dark, the layers of meaning present in old thick walls, and the spirit of nature that is so palpable in Mexico. I was impressed by his great fondness for the little toys and other hand-crafted objects he bought in markets for a few centavos and then photographed in his studio while waiting for customers to show up for portraits. When he photographed the toys he had a sharp eye for details and for what they could tell us about the use and origins of a piece, however small or inexpensive it might be. Faithfully represented, and yet in Weston's personal style, was the sense that each object had a haunting history. He made it easy for me to feel the mystery as well as the mundane side of the life of those who shaped the little forms in clay, straw, or paper.

I spent three months in the colonial city of San Miguel de Allende in 1948, photographing and studying art as an antidote to the stresses caused by working in my family's wholesale hardware distributing business. This very successful business had been founded by my grandfather Van Deren in the nineteenth century. When I returned home in the first weeks of 1946 from service as a naval officer in Okinawa waters, I had not thought out or made plans for the future. I had married during the war, had a young son, and was accustomed as a naval officer to taking orders from superior officers, so I acceded to my father's wish that I, his only son, should join the family business. As captain of a five-thousand-ton tank landing ship (LST), I was well acquainted with efficient ways to unload tightly packed spaces as quickly as possible, so I became operations manager of the warehouses.

I added forklift trucks and roller conveyors to handle railroad carloads of barbwire, kegs of nails, refrigerators, boxes of shotgun shells, and other bulky items distributed to retail hardware stores in the eastern half of Kentucky and adjoining counties of Tennessee and Ohio. I found the challenge satisfying; next I was given the responsibility of directing the company's sales organization. At this I was less successful for the experienced salesmen did not wholly accept my "commanding officer" approach. By the first month of 1948 I was brought into top management of the firm, which meant that I worked directly under my father who was president. I quickly found that his ideas and mine were often at odds.

He had successfully brought the company through the depression and by nature was conservative, whereas I had been given considerable responsibilities as a twenty-two- and twenty-three-year-old naval officer and was inclined to experiment with new ways to do things. I felt the post–World War II period would be one of change in products distributed and markets and wanted to transform the company to meet these challenges. He did not agree to my plan. The differences of opinion caused serious rifts in our relationships in the business and personally, for my wife and I had built a house next to my mother and father's residence out in the country north of Lexington. As a result of the stresses this caused I developed an ulcer and brooded about what the future might hold in store for me if I continued the course I was on.

The doctor I consulted about the ulcer recommended that I get completely away from the immediate problems for some time to get a better perspective on what I should do. I decided Mexico was the place to go to sort out my problems. Just traveling around the country would not give me the time to think through my ideas, yet I did not want merely to sit in the sun and read a few books.

Because I had inherited from my mother an artistic inclination she had seen to it that I took courses in sculpture and design when I was a youngster. This experience and my studies in art history at the University of Kentucky before World War II prompted me to take art courses in one of the art schools then flourishing in San Miguel de Allende. Most of the students were veterans who attended the school under the G.I. Bill, which covered tuition and materials and provided a very small sum for living expenses. I interacted comfortably with these students in a number of classes devoted to the traditional arts. But photography was most important to me because of the time I had spent with Edward Weston and my studies in photographic techniques with a sophisticated photographer who was a retired chemist in Lexington. He had known of Weston's work in California and always held up this master's photographs at the end of a session to serve as a standard of excellence.

In Mexico I took a lot of photographs on my own as well as courses in wood carving, weaving, and lithography. It was at this time that I formulated a plan to concentrate on photographs in Mexico of things and people encountered in the streets, in the markets, and on the plazas.

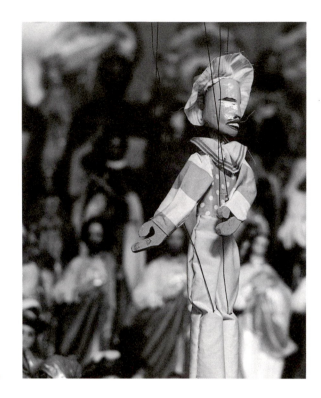

Taxco, Mexico, 1950.

The resulting black-and-white pictures were satisfying and greatly in-creased my fondness for the people whom I got to know in my wanderings in their towns and villages.

In the fall of 1948 I left Mexico and returned to the wholesale hardware business, determined to get along better with my father as a business associate but also determined to do more photography and develop a greater knowledge of the history of the medium as an art form.

This course of action worked reasonably well, but by 1954, when I had become president of the company, I realized I was not going to be happy spending my life as a businessman. I resigned from the company and entered graduate school in the history of art at Indiana University. When it came time to select a thesis topic I expressed a wish to research the influences of photography on nineteenth-century painting, a subject I had already delved into on my own. The proposal was rejected by my committee with the comment that such a focus was inappropriate for an art historian. Members of my committee, all eminent art historians, frankly said the subject did not exist. I was so distressed by this narrow view I switched to sculpture as my major and, under the direction of the very prominent French-American sculptor Robert Laurent, then on the faculty of Indiana University, finished my stay at Indiana with an MFA in sculpture.

In 1958 the chairman of the art department at the University of Florida, Clinton Adams, offered me an appointment as an assistant professor to teach photography and the history of modern art. I accepted. Three years later I joined the faculty at Arizona State University where I taught the same courses. After one year at ASU Clinton Adams, who had become dean of the College of Fine Arts at the University of New Mexico, appointed me director of the university's new art gallery. I also taught creative photography and its history as well as the history of nineteenth- and early twentieth-century art. After a few leaves of absence from UNM to teach art history at St. Martin's School of Art in London and to serve as director of the International Museum of Photography at George Eastman House in Rochester, New York, I eventually became director of the Department of Photography at the San Francisco Museum of Modern Art in 1979.

For the first time since I was a teenager I did not have a darkroom and turned to color photography. I had done some photography using various color films that I could develop myself, but in San Francisco I decided to use Kodachrome, which had to be developed by a Kodak firm, so complex was the process. I found a very able professional printer, Robert Reiter, to make Cibachrome prints for me. This archival material and

Kodachrome are well suited to my sensitivity to the rich colors and dark shadows one encounters in Mexico.

The pictures in this book are the results of concentrated campaigns in Mexico during vacations from my work at the San Francisco Museum of Modern Art from 1979 to 1987 and after I retired to Santa Fe, New Mexico.

My intent was only half-formed when I began to concentrate in 1979 on color photographs of Mexican subjects, especially the people and objects called *folk art* or, more to my liking, *popular arts*. I had long been attracted to the bizarre aspect, or even freakishness, of many Mexican popular arts pieces. Some pieces reveal a wildness, or even a menacing quality in their imagery, which I do not understand but sense is related to the dark side of the cultural history of the Indians. These qualities, even in crude clay pieces, evoke primal energies. Modelled or molded in clay are representations of seemingly ordinary activities that are charged with psychological implications. This type of work makes up perhaps half of the clay pieces I have photographed, not to document them but to create images that represent for me their emotional impact. This goal also applies to tenderly lyrical genre pieces, Catholic religious figures, and amusing works that are somewhat like topical cartoons, all of which reflect some of the characteristics of the Mexican people.

The streets, plazas, and marketplaces of Mexico have traditionally served as business and social gathering places—much more so than people's homes or workplaces. They still do today. Thrown into relief against decaying walls are moments of tragedy, religious and secular rituals, everyday vending, and conversational exchanges. This group of pictures explores the great and interesting variety of objects and activities I have encountered in the older cities and towns.

While there is little of the frenetic hustle and bustle found in American

Taxco, Mexico, 1950.

or European population centers, one quickly feels the inner vitality of the Mexican people. People from various levels of society appear to interact comfortably. It is rare that I feel any estrangement or alienation between poor workers and well-to-do merchants. There is a sense of belonging.

The influences on contemporary Mexican culture are numerous. The Catholic calendar shapes much of Mexican life. Many customs have persisted from pre-Hispanic times: Indians, even when accepting Christianity, maintained a number of their own religious practices. We see this in the popular arts, especially Day of the Dead ceremonies, as well as in fiesta dances and parades.

Then there is the influence of international television. During Corpus Christi in San Miguel de Allende, individuals who participate in the parade celebrating this religious event dress in costumes often based on television or comic book characters. However, beneath the carnival trappings, costumes, and antics are ironical statements or reflections of a societal need to exorcise disturbing experiences or cope with deep-seated fears.

My photographs were artistically conceived, but they also allow us to learn about today's Mexico. Some photographers believe in flinty realism. The realism I seek is flexible; that is, while parts of a photograph may be sharp they are not only a mirror of nature. Explicit imagery does not carry with it enough feeling of *enigma*, which I believe is the essence of art. My major aim has been to turn ordinary events, registered at 1/50th of a second, without the limitation of a specific time or place, into enigmatic or symbolic images that may tell us something about what goes on in people's minds. All kinds of cultural things are revealed—evidences of the effects of international pop movements and fads, as well as the persistence of cultural inheritances from an often dark past.

Seeking to convey my responses to the humanistic qualities I observe in the people of Mexico led me to the use of brightly colored details emerging from dark shadows. This approach also makes it possible to hold together as a unit diverse details that I intend viewers to see as clues to the nature of people's lives and their environments. Only occasionally is there a political subtext to my pictures of people. More often my visual comment is intended to illuminate a facet of everyday life and perhaps catch unconscious gestures that typify a person's activities.

By 1984 I had about one hundred prints that I felt met my criteria as

Pátzcuaro, Mexico, 1952.

"pictures" and that said something I could not articulate but was beginning to feel and understand. I contacted Carmen Masip de Hawkins, a marvelously imaginative and politically savvy administrator in San Miguel de Allende, who is director of the Instituto Nacional de Bellas Artes, and proposed that an exhibition of these prints be held in the school's galleries centrally located in the old city. She was agreeable, and an exhibition was mounted in 1985.

At the opening I talked to many of those who came to the exhibition and found that photographers responded with technical questions. They asked how I did this or that, what film I used, why I did not hold detail in the shadows, and the like. The painters, on the other hand, appreciated the formal qualities, and a number of them quickly grasped what I sought to convey. Mexican viewers were fascinated by familiar subjects that appear in my pictures at odds with their recollections. They said that my photographs showed colors and shapes differently than they had seen them.

A few days after the opening of the exhibition my wife and I were in an arts-and-crafts shop looking at some ceramic pieces and relating them to similar pieces we had recently seen in the city of Guanajuato. An attractive young woman overheard us and asked how she could get to Guanajuato. After we gave her directions she asked our name; when I told her she said, "Oh, you are the photographer who made the pictures at the Bellas Artes. My husband and I were very excited by your work because it is so different from what we are accustomed to seeing in California, where we live." She introduced herself and invited us to join her and her husband for a drink at the place they were renting. (They now own a home in the city and spend there a good deal of time each year.) We accepted and found them to be very interesting people. She is Masako Takahashi, a Japanese-American artist who was brought up surrounded by art, for her family operated Japanese art shops in the San Francisco Bay Area. Her husband is Tony Cohan, a successful author who had recently published *Opium,* a complex historical novel that had been favorably received. As Tony talked about his responses to my pictures I liked what he said, for he had put into words some of my feelings. I subsequently asked him to write the introduction to this book.

Tony was curious about how I went about making my pictures. I told him I never pose a person, rearrange elements, or ask for permission to photograph. This meant I had to develop strategies to conceal my intentions until the moment when I raise the camera to focus and organize the major elements into a picture. I search for a portion of a scene or group of objects that I can bring together as a collection of colors and interesting shapes. In Mexico bright colors are the first thing to attract my eye. I often study a subject, keeping my camera out of sight for some time, before I actually make a photograph. I imagine how colors, people, and objects will fit into an ordered arrangement, for usually I have only a single chance to photograph before a situation changes. My long-standing interest in organizing shapes must meld with what I want to say in human terms before I make an exposure. Form is the substructure which clarifies my aim: to deepen people's understanding of what I see and evoke respect for the people I photograph or the objects they create. I isolate by use of shadows or color contrasts to focus attention on the activities of people and the ways they present things for sale.

I usually try to get away from the sense of a specific place. Rather I seek to convey the spirit of the streets in colonial cities and the weekly markets of villages and towns. In Mexican markets I am initially overwhelmed by moving people, changing spots of color, and patterns of light and shade. The senses are confronted with the smell of flowers, hides, cooking food, and piles of herbs. The jumble of bright colors, buyers and sellers moving through sharply defined dark areas, stimulates an emotional and visual excitement even though the scene may seem banal or prosaic to a Mexican. Gradually the juxtaposed patches of bright color shed their surprises and the spell is broken. I must then control the details of subject matter to capture the feelings I experienced. I am struck in markets by the continuity of age-old customs manifest in selling and buying practices and in personal interchanges on the streets.

One of the pitfalls of recording raw reality with a camera is the amount of detail you inevitably register on film by the very act of pointing a camera and opening the shutter for a fraction of a second. A viewer of photographs can be confused by the plethora of information recorded. A selective view may diminish a photograph's authority as a document, but in using this approach one can create a more telling aesthetic image. Since I am not seeking to document what I see but to convey how I feel about my subjects I use formal devices to concentrate viewer's attention on a person or object that reveals the changes occurring in Mexico as well as the hold traditions continue to have.

172

In broad terms my pictures are an affirmation of my great interest in the way Mexicans interact with each other and the respect I have for their popular arts.

Mine is not a scientific investigation any more than were Gauguin's studies of the South Sea islanders. Gauguin was exploring the effect on people's lives of the interplay between climate, terrain, plentiful food, and the mysterious forces that bring both good fortune and nature's wrath. Through my photographs I seek to comment on social and cultural aspects of life in older parts of Mexico. My pictures call attention to bizarre objects as well as everyday happenings. They reflect both current events and history. Through them we get a widened perspective of how the amalgam of cultures—some with shadowy corners, some rich, some harsh—have produced the stirring culture one finds in Mexico today.

secular and sacred

Designed by Milenda Nan Ok Lee
Typography in Galliard
Typeset by the University of New Mexico Printing Services
Printed by Dai Nippon Printing Company, Ltd.